IMAGES OF DEPARTURE

PADRAIC COLUM

IMAGES
OF
DEPARTURE

THE DOLMEN PRESS

*Set in Plantin type and printed and published
in the Republic of Ireland at The Dolmen Press
Limited, 8 Herbert Place, Dublin 2.*

1969

*Distributed outside Ireland, except in the U.S.A. and Canada
by Oxford University Press*

SBN *196475015*

CONTENTS

IMAGES OF DEPARTURE

The Images of Departure *in this poem are taken from a seventeenth-century Gaelic poem by Thomas Costello addressed to Una MacDermott, and from Orpheus and Eurydice, a statue by John Hughes in the Modern Art Gallery in Dublin. In the first the departure is in pride and anger, in the second it is in reconciliation.*

What recognitions after calendars
Are all unleafed are spreading for me here—
Before these houses in their terraced row!

Each with a fanlight ribbed above the door,
And (emblem of persistence it could be),
A knocker rounded as an iron wreath.

So much! And one thing living from my time
Of eagerness—a laurel by a gate:
Thick-leafed and variegated it still grows;

No leaf is changed since here I came and went,
Or so it seems—but then, whoever saw
A fading laurel by a Dublin lodge? . . .

And if I passed beyond the laurel growth,
And raised the knocker that's an iron wreath,
To stranger who'd appear what would I say?

"And is there one, a student, living here?"
(The words recurring and the heart-beats, too)
And cross the threshold to another door.

A girl rises from beside her books:
She has a name for me that makes a jest
Of greeting, but the greeting finds her eyes.

The oil lamp's radiance fills a world for us;
The books have word of those who are beyond
Brief suns of ours, but who can send a glance

That claims adherence from our breathing selves;
A word so spoken that it stays alone
In citiesful of words; a reaching hand . . .

No girl will rise from her deep arm-chair
And make a jest of greeting; I look towards
Electric glare instead of oil-lamp's glow.

For not beyond the laurel bush I've passed
To speak a stranger at an opened door:
I take a leaf, a scrap of what endured . . .

What was her likeness? It is in the praise
That, turning from his anger, Costello
Bestowed upon MacDermott's downcast child—

"A candlestick of gold upon a queen's
High table, she". But more than stem or branch
Of gold, or tabled treasures was the flame.

And then the voice that went, a rivulet
Where reeds made music, and took current where
The sharpened pebbles made another sound.

But I must thank you, poet, for the rare
Bright figure you upcast before you made
Unblessed departure from old Dermott's house.

You could again into the rush-strewn hall
With only hours at loss. I stand before
A terrace with a name of bygone vogue . . .

          A spacious square,
Somewhat unkempt, is my next journey's end,
A noble's town house, now a gallery.

Through handsome portico I make my way:
People are passing through the lengthy rooms,
Remotely moving, standing without speech;

And I am stayed before the marble pair,
John Hughes's Orpheus and Eurydice:
I knew the sculptor, spoke him once or twice.

Departure here! But not as in the speech
Perpetuated—Costello's proud words—
"My shadow on your street will not be seen".

They have not aged, this pair; they well remember
The eagerness of first companionship,
The dreams, the ardors, and the prophecies.

Her head upon his head, his bowed-down head,
The lyre behind his back, the sentence passed,
But momently the clasp that salves farewell.

The gazers move with recognitions due
To names and figures that are trophies here:
I stand before your marble pair, John Hughes,

To know that, like a bird down on a branch
Stray, unbeckoned, out of a wide sky
Has come to them the moment of accord.

IN SAINT STEPHEN'S GREEN

Bare branches: on the tree above
A nest from seasons gone
That keeps in spite of all that blew
A lone, wild homeliness.

And they that have the lease of it,
Two magpies, flit around;
Their magpie-minds are bent upon
The matter of repair.

Renewal! Like some other beings,
They're claimant of a day
Whose grant is lodging, prospect, store,
Companionship renewed.

The magpies fly with tuft and twig
Up to the nest regained:
Elated by their enterprise
They patch, and probe, and pull.

And in the shadow, not a pair,
A triad: one lets fall
To one below the thread she's spun
Who measures, passes down

To one who's seated: on her lap
The shears, the cutting shears—
Three bronzen women at a task
That is from ancientry.

Like nuns of order so severe
None have remained but they:
They look out on a world where we
A homeliness repair.

EXPECTING NO ONE

The bridge we often crossed, one to the other—
I lean upon its ledge, expecting no one
From north or south, a pilgrim who is mindful
Of all he left behind, and mindful, too,
Of disrepair in all he has come back to.

The seagulls fly up from the darkened river—
Their flight disordered—there is emblem here.

I lean upon the ledge this stilly night—
The word that Thomas Moore has in his song
That's of departures—his statue is within
The watch I keep—the town's worst monument.
No more than he of "banquet hall deserted"
Am I in hope of one to re-appear.

Expecting no one—
Regretting this—that you had come so often
To where I crossed, and that so seldom I,
Moved from set purposes, made a festival
Of your approach, you who were attuned
To all the harps that sounded in the air.
And here I stand with all those purposes
Signed, sealed, delivered as a book in vault,
Between the statue in his metal cloak
And seagulls making their disordered flight,
Expecting no one from the south or north.

DAY'S END

An old woman stands
By her house gable
Calling her chickens—
They run as they're able.

Leghorn, Dorking,
And Plymouth Rock:
They run where she holds
The open crock.

An old man, a poet,
On doorstep, although
No word 's in his mouth
Is calling somehow

On words of deep meaning
That somewhere were said,
On faces like ballads
For street-singers made.

They run; they come to her,
The whole of her flock,
Counting the bantam
Hen and cock.

Evenings ten thousand
Were here and are gone,
Foxes that bear off
This one and that one.

"They're out", says the poet,
Like the flame of the rush-
Candle; they're gone
Like a girl's first blush".

And the old woman's croon
Sounds lonely and far
Like voices that come
Where no footsteps are.

IN THE CARIBBEAN

"Irlanda, O Irlanda,
Irlanda in the sea".
A swallow flew across the deck,
And sang as fleetingly.

One swallow flew; the rowers laid
An oar against a knee,
And raised their heads and looked abroad—
Grey, grey the by-gone sea!

SLEEP AND A LABURNUM TREE

O Sleep, you are as beautiful
As that Laburnum tree
I saw at nightfall in the glen
Where single was the tree,
And solitary the one who saw
Its goldeness become
An offering to the obscure,
Lucent Laburnum!

The tree whose growth is but to droop
Its blossoms near the grass—
And I will say you're beautiful
As that tree is, for all
And all its blooms like candle-shine,
If you will droop on me
Your cob-web blooms, O dark-branched sleep
Before the first bird's call!

BEFORE A ROW OF VOTIVE CANDLES

The candles that before me, placidly
Fulfilling their good office, burn on—
Out of their goodness may they send a gleam
Into my thoughts, my self-exalting thoughts!
O you white witnesses
To things that are above all such rewards
As I cast up and then cast up again:
A gleam spare them,
Or else contain them as I watch you burn
White, shining, prayerful to your votive ends.

SEAN O'DWYER A GLEANNA

His horses, heads uplifted,
Snuff the breeze of morning,
And with expectant glances
Wait the breathed word.

        But Sean O'Dwyer a Gleanna
        The word will not be yours.

His hounds, bred from the noble
Forbears, decry pack's yelping,
But watchful and right-ready
Would hear a ringing voice.

        But, Sean O'Dwyer a Gleanna,
        Your voice will not reach them.

The oak-trees in his manor
Deep-rooted as his race is,
Has heard the stroke of axes
Come near as are their leaves.

        But where will Sean O'Dwyer
        Get tidings of their fall?

The sheath his broad-sword 's worn,
The harp that roused his fathers,
The great cup that we pledged from
Are relics in his hall.

        But, Sean O'Dwyer a Gleanna,
        Is laid beside the Boyne.

AFTER SPEAKING OF ONE WHO DIED A LONG TIME BEFORE

"She should have had", I said, and then I stopped.
Knowing her want, how could I speak of it—
I who have only words of men befriended.
I should have had the language used by men
Who stood outside their tents, the waste before them,
And looking towards a great star made a poem
Of tenderness and grief, all manliness—
The words as lonely as their desert marches—
I should have had possession of that tongue
To make it known, the haplessness, the loss
Of one who went into a life forsaken.

And there were men in Ireland, annalists,
Unfailing men for whom all things had failed,
Whose chronicle was pillage would destroy
The vellum that they wrote on and make blank
A thousand years a people could take pride in,
And on a page that was the volume's end
Wrote of a personal loss, a wife or child
Dead, in words that have eventfulness
Being taken off the loom of history:
I should have had reversion of such words
To speak of all she lost in her life's decades.
"She should have had", you said, touched by what held me
"The simple things that we will always have".

FORGET ME NOTS

Among the tulips and the aspholdels
The small blue flowers, the groundlings of the garden,
Whose name you bring to me, forget-me-nots.

And I had seen their semblance stitched upon
A brim of hat by one who scarcely knew
A holiday from year's end to year's end,
The stiffened blooms of blue, a counter's leavings,
And she would wear them as a badge of fortune,
Leaving the drabness of a room for feast-day,
The eager look beneath her brim of hat.
And in your Magian garden here I stand
Discerning one-day fortune of the poor,
The mindful flowers, the small forget-me-nots
Beside the tulips and the aspholdels.

JUDGMENT

Then you will judge—No, no, you'll not accuse:
Erect you'll stand as when the judgment given
Concerned yourself, your wildness and your grace,
And you will say, "There is a place of sorrow
For all was lost in this not hopeless world—
There go and grieve for my ungifted days".
In lamb's wool garb you'll stand erect and judge,
No lily nor no taper in your hand,
But with the remnant of a love stitched up
To make a napkin for that crying face.
Yet you will judge, for judgment must be given—
The Maker of the World willed it so.

NAME AND LEGEND

The seagulls fly around the tower,
And range that 's higher claim,
Where you have come, enchanting child,
Filled with a poet's name.

A name! What name? Once on a time
Someone of lucky growth
Was imaged in the syllables
That leave you all but mute.

Someone there was who could distrain
Words that had pulse and gleam
Was imaged in the syllables
You say as in a dream.

A legend now as of a star
That's there but no more seen,
And you have come, enchanting child
To gaze where glow has been.

Look where you've come! Old scripts, old scrolls,
Old laurels, huddle here,
And there, like shells, medallions,
Their features falsely clear.

Look! Higher than the seagulls glide
The dusky swifts ascend—
Until the vault of sky they reach
Their journey has no end.

Go with the swifts, you child of grace—
They sleep on open wings,
And dream of all that fare below
As of beloved things.

Dream of me there in stirless air,
Beyond the seagull's range,
Above enshadowed beings we name
Time and Loss and Change.

THEN I WAS MAD

Then I was mad, and truly mad,
As mad as any clown
That all in rags, with sooty face
Goes crassly through a town.

None hindered me; through windows lit
I saw as I went by,
A cradle rocked, a table spread,
A man stare drunkenly.

And it was curious, I thought,
Such motions still were made:
A girl pinned a nosegay on,
A lad a fiddle played.

The dealer in the step-down shop
Who saw me, did not fail
To make them weigh down evenly,
The two sides of her scale.

And where the bake-house stands I stopped:
I let the minutes pass;
The night was pleasant all around,
So fresh a smell there was.

The ovens then were opening
For bread with fragrance fused:
Van after van I'd send, I thought
To men who were refused

Bread. I knew myself refused
More, more! I bided there;
With bended head I took the draught
Left over from despair.

The statue of the Emperor
Stands in its pride of place,
No madness breaks the nobleness
That 's moulded in his face.

No sign is there of that blind night
I flung my wits away,
And seized on core that would not shake,
On purpose that would stay.

O Time! Again you have betrayed
Impulse to history.
With your retarding leaves between
Instant and destiny.

I ask this riddle of myself—
Myself no answer sends:
And could the madness of that night
Bespeak my ordered ends!

THE DYING GAUL

Propped from the proneness that his brow bends towards
With hand and knee, the stricken warrior
Keeps pulse to ransom moments round his heart.

Ungarbed: the one arrayment left to him
Is twisted metal banded round his neck—
Gold it would be—the torque that leaves a name

To conqueror's lineage and that marks him one
Of those impetuous, unholding men,
The Celts, the Gauls who Delphi took and Rome.

The sculptor who gave this death-nearing man
A statue's life, gave it identity,
Carving the lineaments that we recognise

Amongst the kindred by Atlantic shore
In these our days removed from name of Gaul,
Parnassian Delphi or Italic Rome.

Two mighty stones and one that's laid across
Their monument to some torque-wearing King—
The Giant's Grave, they, historyless, proclaim.

THE BOOK OF KELLS

First, make a letter like a monument—
An upright like the fast-held hewn stone
Immovable, and half-rimming it
The strength of Behemoth his neck-bone,
And underneath that yoke, a staff, a rood
Of no less hardness than the cedar wood.

Then, on a page made golden as the crown
Of sainted man, a scripture you enscroll
Black, firmly, with the quickened skill
Lessoned by famous masters in our school,
And with an ink whose lustre will keep fresh
For fifty generations of our flesh.

And limn below it the Evangelist
In raddled coat, on bench abidingly,
Simple and bland: Matthew his name or Mark,
Or Luke or John; the book is by his knee,
And thereby its similitudes: Lion,
Or Calf, or Eagle, or Exalted Man.

The winds that blow around the world—the four
Winds in their colours on your pages join—
The Northern Wind—its blackness interpose;
The Southern Wind—its blueness gather in;
In redness and in greenness manifest
The splendours of the Winds of East and West.

And with these colours on a ground of gold
Compose a circuit will be seen by men
As endless patience, but is nether web
Of endless effort—a strict pattern:
Illumination lighting interlace
Of cirque and scroll, of panel and lattice.

A single line describes them and enfolds,
One line, one course where term there is none,
Which in its termlessness is envoying
The going forth and the return one.
With man and beast and bird and fish therein
Transformed to species that have never been.

With mouth a-gape or beak a-gape each stands
Initial to a verse of miracle,
Of mystery and of marvel (Depth of God!)
That Alpha or Omega may not spell,
Then, finished with these wonders and these signs,
Turn to the figure of your first outlines.

Axal, our angel, has sustained you so
In hand, in brain; now to him seal that thing
With figures many as the days of man,
And colours, like the fire's enamelling—
That baulk, that letter you have greatly reared
To stay the violence of the entering Word!

TO DAME MARGOT FONTEYN

Silence and flight! And then there is
The motion of the reeds,
And you who poetry of words
Withhold can give us these.

The seagull when she leaves behind
The elemental sea
Veers with unearthly grace above
Our roofs, and silently.

Silence and flight! More magical
Than water from the Well
At the World's end, your offering
All that is not ourselves.

WILD DUCK

A wild duck flies across the sky,
Alone, resolved, enskyed,
Distance-entailed: an image here
To hearten all my ways,
So, when I meet a Councillor,
A Poet, or a General,
I'll tell him ere he says
His say with rhyme and reason gibbed,
"A wild duck flies above the town
Alone, resolved, enskyed!"

NEAR LEGEND

Place names in some Irish county
Sometimes yield a trace of legend:
Thus we read about some tribesman
Who arrives and does a service
For a king or for a blacksmith,
Leaves a name to pool or pasture,
Then is gone where no one knows him—
Like the corncrake in the meadow
Who departs when scythe 's in grasses.

    So in that unpaged narration,
The itinerary that 's my lifetime,
One appears, is somehow noted,
Then goes out of ken for all time.

    We were strangers in that borough:
No one came upon our doorstep,
No child claimed the right to play with
Us, the children here transported.

    In the yard that we had lease of
There was heritage from someone
Who had dealings with seafarers:
Broken row-boat, planks outlasting
Purpose that no one could tell of,
And a figurehead whose human
Visage told she was abandoned.

    Into yard that we had lease of
He came without leave or licence.
Was he swarthy? Tall? 'tis likely;
Bearded? Yes, like king in card-pack,

But the adze upon his shoulder
Was the badge by which I mind him.
　　　Like a man whose blow's a portent
He struck adze upon the row-boat,
Struck again and left it splinters.
Not abating blows he ripped up
Planks and left them heaps of splinters.
Then the figurehead he turned to,
Raised the adze up to his shoulder,
Struck his blow, his weightiest, on her—
Struck, and struck a blow more weighty—
Left her neither head nor figure.
　　　We stood by and watched the stranger.
"Now", he said when ceased the onset,
"You have firewood till nigh Christmas".
She came to herself, our mother,
Who had stood there like a statue.
Lifting pot that had geranium
In full bloom, she brought it to him
As thank-offer for his labour.
"No", he said, "I take no payment,
What my adze can do is given".

Such a one as he is noted
By one pious towards old places,
Noted once, and rightly noted,
Since one rarely, king or blacksmith,
Meets one in a town or parish
Self-determined, self-rewarding,
Adze or no adze on his shoulder.

DISCOVERY

I lay upon a bank of grass
In idleness. No sight was there
To make me wonder or rejoice:
My gaze was on the town forenenst:
No house was there but was the same
As house beside; the steeple, too—
It was so spare it scanted bird
Would perch on it. And there I lay.
Of houses like and steeple spare
I was unrapt discoverer.

And then, not listening yet, I heard
A murmur and a rumour near:
The bees I'd seen in flight, on flower
Were in a throng. And could it be
That they had lodging in the ground?
I raised the moss, their parapet,
And saw the galleries that drew
The scores and scores, and then I saw
The edifice whose fame was in
The rumour I had chanced to hear,
And then was I discoverer!

Years have gone by like flight of drones,
Droning away. Still, as I chance
On lawn or sward, I bend my wits
To hear a murmur, rumour near,
And be again discoverer!
That amber town that's always filled,
Always deserted by its tribes!

AUSTRALIAN TREE

I went around my brother's house,
And it was winter there,
But winter in Australia . . .
The sky was summer-blue,
And folded in that graciousness
A tree, a single tree.

How would it seem if speech of mine
Broke instantly in verse,
Stanza on stanza, rhyme on rhyme,
Sultanas, brides, gazelles?
No less a wonder was that tree—
Unleafed its branches, unleafed all,
But on their starkness grew—
Ridges of bloom, above, below—
The red that 's forged to flame.

I mused, "a generation spared
Elders and monitors;
No leaves, no buds, exemplars:
The Flame Tree its name."

The Flame Tree and black swans I've seen
In our Antipodes.

And at its butt that owlish bird,
The Kookaburra sat,
Impassively as though to say
"Nothing to wonder at!"

P6